GRAINS
Are Good For You!

by
Gloria Koster

PEBBLE
a capstone imprint

Published by Pebble, an imprint of Capstone
1710 Roe Crest Drive
North Mankato, Minnesota 56003
capstonepub.com

Library of Congress Cataloging-in-Publication Data
Names: Koster, Gloria, author.
Title: Grains are good for you! / by Gloria Koster.
Description: North Mankato, Minnesota : Pebble, [2023] | Series: Healthy
foods | Includes bibliographical references and index. | Audience: Ages
5-8 | Audience: Grades K-1 | Summary: "Bread, cereal, and quinoa . . .
These healthy foods are all part of the grain group! In this Pebble Explore
book, learn where grains come from, what nutrition they provide, and how
they help form a healthy diet. Filled with fantastic facts, including grain
alternatives, curious young readers-and report writers-will have plenty to
digest"-- Provided by publisher.
Identifiers: LCCN 2022008206 (print) | LCCN 2022008207 (ebook) |
    ISBN 9781666351262 (hardcover) | ISBN 9781666351323 (paperback) |
    ISBN 9781666351385 (pdf) | ISBN 9781666351507 (kindle edition)
Subjects: LCSH: Grain in human nutrition--Juvenile literature.
Classification: LCC QP144.G73 K67 2023 (print) | LCC QP144.G73 (ebook) |
DDC 641.3/31--dc23/eng/20220602
LC record available at https://lccn.loc.gov/2022008206
LC ebook record available at https://lccn.loc.gov/2022008207

Editorial Credits
Editor: Donald Lemke; Designer: Tracy Davies; Media Researcher:
Julie De Adder; Production Specialist: Katy LaVigne

Image Credits
Getty Images: AleaImage, 7, Ariel Skelley, 20, filadendron, 5,
GoodLifeStudio, 15, helovi, 19, Hispanolistic, 27, Jose Luis Pelaez Inc,
13, Katrina Wittkamp, 18, mediaphotos, 23, nicolesy, cover (front),
SeventyFour, 12; Shutterstock: Africa Studio, 28, Alena Bahdanovich,
16, BasPhoto, 14, beboy, 17, Daisy Daisy, 26, Frolova_Elena, 6, Iasmina
Calinciuc, 8, Iraida Bearlala (background), cover and throughout,
lightwavemedia, 4, Losangela, 24, Monkey Business Images, 29, Natasha
Pankina (doodles), cover and throughout, Ohn Mar (doodles), cover and
throughout, Olga Nayashkova, 25, Scharfsinn, 21, Tefi, 9, Vectorgoods
studio, (popcorn doodle), cover, 1; USDA: 11

All internet sites appearing in back matter were available and accurate
when this book was sent to press.

TABLE OF CONTENTS

Words in **bold** are defined in the glossary.

WHAT ARE GRAINS?

Did you have cereal for breakfast? Will you eat a sandwich for lunch? Is spaghetti on the dinner menu? Then you are eating grains!

Oats are grains often found in cereal. Wheat is a grain used to make bread. People make pasta from wheat, rice, or barley. These are just a few types of grains.

Grains come from grassy plants. These plants have seeds. People dry the seeds to be used as grains.

Grains come in different shapes and sizes. Some seeds are tiny. Some are much larger, like popcorn kernels.

wheat grains

white rice and brown rice

There are two kinds of grains: whole grains and **refined** grains. Whole grains are the healthiest kind. That's because whole grains have all three parts of the grain seed.

Refined grains have only one part of the seed, the endosperm. The bran and germ are removed. This type of grain is often ground into flour. Flour is used to make bread, cake, pizza, and more.

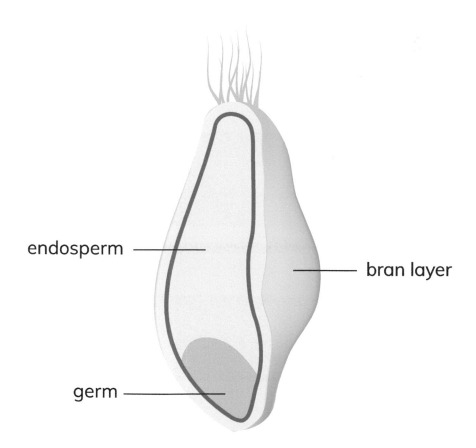

endosperm ——————

bran layer

germ ——————

GRAINS KEEP US HEALTHY

MyPlate is a guide for healthy meals. Half your plate should have fruits and vegetables. Half should have **protein** foods and grains. A small amount of dairy is on the side.

Grains are one of the largest parts!

That's because grains have many **vitamins** and minerals. Vitamins and minerals are **nutrients**. Nutrients keep you healthy and help you grow.

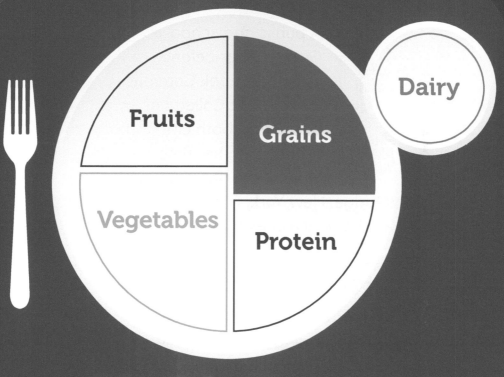

MyPlate.gov

Grains are healthy foods for many reasons. Grains have **carbohydrates**. Some people call these "carbs."

Carbs are a kind of sugar. They give you energy to play and work.

Grains also have **fiber**. What's that? Fiber is the rough part of food that your body can't break down, or **digest**.

Fiber makes you feel full. It also helps other foods pass through your body.

GROWING GRAINS

People have eaten grains for thousands of years. Grains used to mostly grow wild. Now they are often planted. They make one crop a year.

Early peoples grew grains.

Farmers harvest corn.

Grains grow around the world. In some countries, grains are the most common foods.

rye field

Different grains need different **climates** to grow. Wheat grows best in warm and sunny areas. Another type of grain is rye. Rye grows best in cooler places, like Germany and Russia.

Parts of Asia are perfect for rice. The weather there is often hot and **humid**.

Rice grows in a wet field called a paddy. At harvest, the farmer drains the paddy. Then the farmer takes seeds from the plants. The rice is the seed.

rice paddy

ears of corn

Oats and corn grow well in the United States. Farmers often plant these crops in the middle part of the country. It is known as the Great Plains.

This area has a **temperate** climate. The summers are warm. The winters are cold.

Sorghum is another type of grain. It needs a dry climate. That's why parts of Africa are perfect for growing this kind of grain.

sorghum

Grains feed people around the world. Animals eat grains too! Farmers feed corn, wheat, and sorghum to their **livestock**.

    People use grains for more than food. Grains are made into oil for cooking. Some grains, like corn, are used to make fuel. This fuel runs cars and machines.

MAKING SMART CHOICES

Go grocery shopping with a grown-up. Look at the food labels and packaging. Find foods with healthy whole grains.

Many snack foods are made with grains. Crackers, cookies, and sugary cereals all contain grains. These foods often have a lot of sugar and fat too. Don't eat them too often.

quinoa salad

Taste some new foods! How about **quinoa**? Some people call it a "superfood." That's because quinoa is packed with nutrients. It has protein too.

Use brown rice instead of white rice. Toss barley into stew. Make some buckwheat pancakes.

Having a pizza night? Try a whole wheat crust!

Some grains have **gluten**. Not everyone can eat gluten. It makes them feel sick.

Gluten is in wheat. It is also in barley and rye. Rice, corn, and oats do not have gluten.

If you can't have gluten, be careful.
Read food labels. Going out to eat?
Ask for a gluten-free meal.

Try to eat enough grains every day.
Don't forget to get lots of exercise
too! Biking, running, and sports are
excellent ways to stay healthy and fit.

These activities and whole grains
will help keep you healthy and strong!

GLOSSARY

carbohydrate (kar-boh-HYE-drate)—a substance found in grains that gives people energy

climate (KLYE-mit)—the usual weather in a place

digest (dye-JEST)—to break down foods in the stomach and organs, so it can be used in the body

fiber (FYE-bur)—a part of foods, such as fruits and vegetables, that helps foods move through the intestines

gluten (GLOO-tuhn)—a part of wheat and flour that holds dough together

humid (HYOO-mid)—damp and moist

livestock (LIVE-stok)—animals raised on a farm or ranch, such as horses, sheep, and cows

nutrient (NOO-tree-uhnt)—part of food that is needed for growth and health

protein (PRO-teen)—one type of nutrient found in food

quinoa (KEEN-wah)—starchy seeds which are used as food and ground into flour

refined (rih-FYND)—free of something unwanted

temperate (TEM-pur-it)—a place with neither very high nor very low temperatures

vitamin (VYE-tuh-min)—a nutrient in food that works along with minerals to keep us healthy

READ MORE

Schuh, Mari. *Food Is Fuel*. North Mankato, MN: Capstone, 2020.

Schwartz, Heather E. *Cookie Monster's Foodie Truck: A Sesame Street Celebration of Food*. Minneapolis: Lerner Publications, 2020.

Webster, Christy. *Follow That Food!* New York: Random House, 2021.

INTERNET SITES

Harvard School of Public Health: "The Nutrition Source" hsph.harvard.edu/nutritionsource/what-should-you-eat/whole-grains/

Healthy Kids Association: "Grains, Breads & Cereals" healthy-kids.com.au/food-nutrition/5-food-groups/breads-cereals/

USDA MyPlate: "Grains" myplate.gov/eat-healthy/grains

INDEX

ABOUT THE AUTHOR

A public and school librarian, Gloria Koster belongs to the Children's Book Committee of Bank Street College of Education. She enjoys both city and country life, dividing her time between Manhattan and the small town of Pound Ridge, New York. Gloria has three adult children and a bunch of energetic grandkids.